VOLUME 3 **IRON**

WONDER WOMAN

VOLUME 3 IRON

BRIAN **AZZARELLO** writer

CLIFF **CHIANG** artist

TONY **AKINS** DAN **GREEN** GORAN **SUDŽUKA**
AMILCAR **PINNA** RICK **BURCHETT**
additional artists

MATTHEW **WILSON** colorist
NICK **FILARDI** additional colors

JARED K. **FLETCHER** letterer

CLIFF **CHIANG** original series & collection cover artist

WONDER WOMAN created by WILLIAM MOULTON **MARSTON**

MATT IDELSON Editor – Original Series CHRIS CONROY Associate Editor – Original Series
RACHEL PINNELAS Editor ROBBIN BROSTERMAN Design Director – Books
ROBBIE BIEDERMAN Publication Design

BOB HARRAS Senior VP – Editor-in-Chief, DC Comics

DIANE NELSON President DAN DIDIO and JIM LEE Co-Publishers
GEOFF JOHNS Chief Creative Officer
JOHN ROOD Executive VP – Sales, Marketing and Business Development
AMY GENKINS Senior VP – Business and Legal Affairs NAIRI GARDINER Senior VP – Finance
JEFF BOISON VP – Publishing Planning MARK CHIARELLO VP – Art Direction and Design
JOHN CUNNINGHAM VP – Marketing TERRI CUNNINGHAM VP – Editorial Administration
ALISON GILL Senior VP – Manufacturing and Operations HANK KANALZ Senior VP – Vertigo and Integrated Publishing
JAY KOGAN VP – Business and Legal Affairs, Publishing JACK MAHAN VP – Business Affairs, Talent
NICK NAPOLITANO VP – Manufacturing Administration SUE POHJA VP – Book Sales
COURTNEY SIMMONS Senior VP – Publicity BOB WAYNE Senior VP – Sales

WONDER WOMAN VOLUME 3: IRON

DC Comics, 1700 Broadway, New York, NY 10019
A Warner Bros. Entertainment Company.
Printed by RR Donnelley, Salem, VA, USA. 8/09/13. First Printing.

HC ISBN: 978-1-4012-4261-9
SC ISBN: 978-1-4012-4607-5

SUSTAINABLE FORESTRY INITIATIVE Certified Chain of Custody
At Least 20% Certified Forest Content
www.sfiprogram.org
SFI-01042
APPLIES TO TEXT STOCK ONLY

Library of Congress Cataloging-in-Publication Data

Azzarello, Brian.
Wonder Woman. Volume 3, Iron / Brian Azzarello, Cliff Chiang, Tony Akins.
pages cm
"Originally published in single magazine form in Wonder Woman 13-18."
ISBN 978-1-4012-4261-9
1. Graphic novels. I. Chiang, Cliff. II. Akins, Tony. III. Title. IV. Title: Iron.
PN6728.W6A99 2013
741.5'973—dc23
2013016905

DC COMICS proudly presents BEFORE THE NEW 52!
INCONCEIVABLY CONCEIVED ON A MYSTERIOUS ISLAND VOID OF MEN THAT WOMEN CALL PARADISE,
SHE IS KNOWN AS *PRINCESS DIANA*--DAUGHTER OF THE MIGHTY *QUEEN HIPPOLYTA*, RULER OF THE AMAZONS!
BUT HER MOTHER HOLDS A SECRET--THAT DIANA'S FATHER IS *ZEUS*--THE KING OF THE GODS!
NO ONE KNOWS THIS--NOT EVEN US, WHO CALL HER...*WONDER WOMAN*!

THE LAIR OF THE
MINOTAUR!

*T*HE MONTHLY MONSTER STRIKES AGAIN! RATHER THAN GIVE *WONDER WOMAN'S MERRY MEN* THEIR MARCHING ORDERS, WE DUG UP A STORY FROM *WONDER WOMAN'S* PAST! MAY YOU ENJOY THIS MAGNIFICENT MISSIVE THAT ORIGINALLY APPEARED IN *"ALL-GIRL ADVENTURE TALES FOR MEN #41"*

MY PRIZE IS NEARLY IN MY GRASP. THOUGH MY ARMS DO ACHE AS ATLAS' MUST, I SHAN'T GIVE UP MY QUEST!

story & art by
BRIAN   **CLIFF**
"KISS MY" & *"CHUMP"*
AZZARELLO   **CHIANG**

coloring
"MUDDY" MATT WILSON
lettering
"JITTERY" JARED FLETCHER

...AND THE **AMAZONS!** THE FIERCE TRIBE OF WARRIOR WOMEN WHO SHUN THE **WORLD OF MAN!**

DIANA, IT IS I, **QUEEN HIPPOLYTA--** YOUR **MOTHER!** WE HAVE BEEN AWAITING YOUR RETURN--AND THE PRIZE YOU MUST DELIVER!

QUEEN HIPPOLYTA'S TONE MASKS HER CONCERN...FOR SHE KNOWS THAT MANY YOUNG AMAZONS **FAIL** IN THEIR QUESTS...

TODAY IS YOUR BIRTHDAY...

AS IS OUR CUSTOM, YOU NEED TO PRESENT ME WITH A **SUITABLE PRESENT,** OR THE PASSING OF YOUR YEAR WILL **NOT** BE ACKNOWLEDGED.

MY QUEEN, FORGIVE ME. ALL I COULD FIND...

...IS A **HARPY'S EGG!**

HOORAY FOR PRINCESS DIANA!

FROM THE SHADOWS AN OMINOUS FIGURE DRAPED IN VULTURE PLUMES STANDS IN WATCH...

THE GIRL EXHIBITS SKILLS FAR BEYOND HER YOUNG AGE...

PERHAPS **SHE** IS THE ONE...

LATER THAT NIGHT, THE AMAZON CITY OF **THEMYSCIRA** CELEBRATES THEIR PRINCESS'S BIRTHDAY WITH A GRAND FEAST--COMPLETE WITH **GAMES OF MARTIAL SKILL!**

AN ODD REQUEST IS MADE...

MY QUEEN, MAY THE PRINCESS AND I DEMONSTRATE WHAT WE'VE LEARNED IN OUR TRAINING EXERCISES?

BUT...WE ARE NOT OLD ENOUGH FOR THE GAMES!

METHINKS I WOULD LIKE THAT, **ALEKA**-- BUT WITH WOODEN SWORDS. I DO NOT WANT TO SEE ONE OF YOU INJURED.

PITY THAT BE **EXACTLY** WHAT THE QUEEN WILL SEE...

THE COMBAT **BEGINS!**

GREAT HERA!

ALEKA IS COMING AT ME WITH **ALL** HER MIGHT!

ALEKA IS FIGHTING FOR REAL--MEANING *I'D* BETTER, TOO! I DO NOT WISH TO HURT HER THOUGH, SO PERHAPS IF I...

THHWACK

YIELD?

NEVER! I AM A *TRUE AMAZON WARRIOR!*

NOT *YET* YOU'RE NOT!

WELL, YOU WILL *NEVER* BE...

CLAY!

THE MUD STINGS, BUT NOT AS MUCH AS ALEKA'S WORDS...

...WORDS THAT SEND THE PRINCESS *INTO A RAGE!*

TAKE IT *BACK!*

¿KOFF¿

YIELD!

¿KOFF¿

DAUGHTER, *STOP!* YOU'RE *HURTING* HER!

I--

I'M SORRY!

DIANA RUNS INTO THE FOREST AS FAR AS HER LEGS WILL CARRY HER BEFORE FALLING ON THE BANKS OF A SILENT STREAM...

WHAT DID I DO TO DESERVE SUCH A FATE? TO BE FORMED FROM CLAY-- TO NOT HAVE REAL PARENTS-- TO NEVER FIT IN!!*

*DIANA DOESN'T KNOW THA SHE DOES HAVE A MOTHER AN A FATHER--QUEEN HIPPOLYT AND ZEUS, KING OF OLYMPUS -MALIGNANT MAT

I MAY LOOK LIKE MY SISTERS, BUT I WILL NEVER BE LIKE THEM-- AND THEY WILL ALWAYS KNOW THAT IN THEIR HEARTS!

WHY MUST I BE DIFFERENT?

DRIP

PERHAPS, PRINCESS...

HEARING A STRANGE VOICE, DIANA RESPONDS AS HER AMAZON TRAINING HAS TAUGHT HER!

...IT IS A GIFT TO BE DIFFERENT.

WHO ARE YOU TO SAY SUCH A THING?

HA! HAST THOU SPENT ALL THY TIME IN THE ARENA AND NONE IN THE TEMPLE? TRULY THOU ART AFTER MINE OWN HEART!

LITTLE ONE, I BE AN OLYMPIAN. I BE THE SETTLER OF DISPUTE. I BE *BLOOD!* I BE *GUTS!* I BE *IRON!*

I BE WAR!

AND I BE HERE WITH AN OFFER...

THOU HAST BEEN TRAINED BY *AMAZONS*-- BRAVE WARRIORS, TRUE--BUT THERE IS *MORE* TO LEARN. *WARRIOR WAYS,* THAT ONLY A *GOD* CAN TEACH.

I *WANT* TO LEARN!

EXCELLENT! HERE IN THE FOREST BEYOND YONDER WALLS EACH FULL MOON, I WILL MAKETH THE GREATEST WARRIOR THE WORLD HAS SEEN OUT OF THEE!

AND SO EVERY MONTH, DIANA MEETS THE OLYMPIAN UNDER THE **FULL MOON**. THERE HE TEACHES HER TO HARNESS HER **BODY**...

AND HER **SPIRIT**...

TO BE **ONE** WITH THE WAYS OF **WAR**!

SPLENDID, LITTLE ONE!

AND WAR IS **PROUD**, FOR DIANA'S SKILLS RIVAL THOSE OF BOTH BRAVE **ULYSSES** AND BRAWNY **ACHILLES**--COMBINED!

SHE BRINGS THE IMMORTAL SOMETHING AKIN TO JOY, AND FOR A BRIEF MOMENT HE ALLOWS HIMSELF TO DREAM OF REST, AND OF ONE DAY PASSING ON THE MANTLE.

ALL THE WHILE, DIANA NEVER NEGLECTS HER TRADITIONAL AMAZON STUDIES.

SHE PROVES HERSELF **STRONGER** AND **FASTER** THAN THE OTHER GIRLS HER AGE.

AS WELL AS SOME OF HER AMAZON TEACHERS!

MY PRECIOUS DAUGHTER, YOU DO ME PROUD. YOU WILL MAKE A FINE **QUEEN**, ONE DAY...

A YEAR PASSES.

THOU DID WELL TONIGHT. WE'LL CELEBRATE AS WARRIORS, WITH *MEAD* FROM *MARKISAN*-- TRULY THE FINEST FERMENTER FROM THIS OR *ANY* ERA!

I WANT TO USE A BLADE.

EH?

WOOD IS FOR *CHILDREN.*

LITTLE ONE...STEEL IS REAL. A BLADE IN ONE'S HAND IS TRUTH--AND LIKE IT, MUST BE USED AS SUCH.

IT MUST BE RELENTLESS, UNERRING, AND UNFORGIVING.

THOU KNOW *NOT* WHAT YOU *ASK.*

I *DO.* I WANT TO USE REAL BLADES.

⸲SIGH⸲ SO BE IT. THIS IS THY CHOICE. THE NEXT MOON, WE *FIGHT...*

...TO THE *DEATH!*

WHAT!?

DO NOT PICK UP A SWORD AGAINST A MAN UNLESS YOU MEAN TO PUT HIM *DOWN* WITH IT. *THAT* IS THE *WARRIOR'S WAY.*

UNDERSTOOD?

I UNDERSTAND.

THE BATTLE IS JOINED! IT LASTS FOR HOURS!

LATER, THE AMAZONS WOULD SPEAK OF UNEXPLAINABLE LIGHTNING FLASHING FROM THE MOUNTAINTOP-- SO FIERCE IS THE CLASH OF REAL ON STEEL!

ONE MONTH LATER...

AN ENTIRE YEAR HATH PASSED! AS IT BE THINE *THIRTEENTH* BIRTH DAY, THOU MUST BRING THY MOTHER *TRIBUTE.* THEREIN LIES THE GREATEST TREASURE OF ALL FOR THE TAKING-- IF THOU *DARE!*

I'M READY FOR *ANY* CHALLENGE!

SO BE IT.

TWIXT YONDER TWIN MONOLITHS THOU SHALT WRITE THY LEGEND!

WONDER HOW I NEVER NOTICED THEM BEFORE...

DIANA FINDS A SMALL OPENING IN THE ROCKS...

I WILL MAKE YOU PROUD, WAR.

I HAVE NO DOUBT OF THAT, LITTLE ONE.

THIS IS NOT A CAVE, BUT SOME SORT OF ANCIENT UNDERGROUND *LABYRINTH!* WHY WAS NO MENTION MADE OF IT IN MY AMAZONIAN STUDIES?

GREAT HERA!

AS THEY GROW ACCUSTOM TO THE DANK DARKNESS, DIANA'S EYES ANSWER HER QUESTION! HER HAIR STANDS ON END-- THIS IS A PLACE OF *GREAT DANGER!*

A PLACE WHERE THOSE WHO ENTER...

NEVER LEAVE!

GOOD THING I TIED MY MAGIC LASSO TO A ROCK AT THE OPENING, SO I CAN FIND MY WAY OUT!

THE BRAVE YOUNG PRINCESS TRAVELS DEEPER AND DEEPER INTO THE TWISTING MAZE...

THE AIR GETS FOULER WITH EACH STEP I TAKE...

NOTHING BUT DUST AND COBWEBS. WAR SAID I'D FIND TREASURE HERE...

WHAT COULD HE HAVE MEANT?

CLOP

WHEN DIANA TURNS, THE BLOOD IN HER VEINS GOES ICIER THAN THE SEA SHE PLUNGED INTO A YEAR AGO!

RRRRGGGRR

GREAT HERA!

THE MINOTAUR!

YES!--THE MINOTAUR-- THE MOST FEARSOME BEAST KNOWN TO MAN, WOMAN, OR GOD!

WAR MUST HAVE TRANSPORTED US TO CRETE! THAT EXPLAINS WHY I'D NEVER SEEN THE MONOLITHS BEFORE!

IT BE FURY IMPOSSIBLE TO TAME! MURDEROUS RAGE IN ITS PUREST FORM!

ITS LIFE'S MISSION--TO KILL!

OOF!

NO--MY LANTERN!

KRAK

BWAARGH

FWOOOM

THAT WAS THE PROVERBIAL LUCKY BREAK...

KKIIIILLL!

IT'S TOO STRONG... SURELY I CANNOT BEST THE BEAST IN COMBAT!

IN ITS BLIND RAGE, THE RAVENOUS MINOTAUR DOESN'T NOTICE WHAT IT'S STEPPED INTO-- DIANA'S *MAGIC LASSO!*

GOT YOU!

CRASH

IT'S NO USE! I'M JUST MAKING HIM ANGRIER!

WAIT! THAT'S IT!

A CLEVER WARRIOR...

...USES HER OPPONENT'S WEAPON...

RrRAAOOoW

...AGAINST THEM!

AS THE MINOTAUR *CHARGES*, DIANA LEAPS AWAY--CAUSING THE BERSERK BRUTE TO HURL HEAD-FIRST INTO THE HARD *STONE WALL* SHE'D BACKED UP AGAINST!

SMAAAASH

IT *WORKED!* HE'S DAZED!

TIME TO *FINISH THE JOB!*

WHUMP

I *DID IT!* I VANQUISHED THE *MIGHTY MINOTAUR!*

YOU HATH, AND WORDS CANNOT EXPRESS THE *ADMIRATION* I FEEL...

WHAT?!

DO *NOT* FAIL THIS TASK, WARRIOR! THINE ENEMIES MUST BE *ELIMINATED*, LEST THEY RETURN FOR THINE *OWN* HEAD!

REVENGE IS *NOT* AN OPTION TO LEAVE A FOE!

THOU WISHES TO BE A WARRIOR? A *TRUE WARRIOR* SHOWS *NO MERCY!*

BUT *WAR*, THAT NIGHT ON THE MOUNTAINTOP...

YOU DID.

THE PURPOSE OF WAR IS TO *END* CONFLICT. YOU *MUST* STRIKE.

I WILL *NOT* KILL. NOT LIKE *THIS.*

LITTLE ONE, DOST THOU *REMEMBER* WHAT IT MEANS TO *RAISE* A SWORD AGAINST A *MAN?*

...YES.

AND WAR BELLOWS-- NOT WITH THE RAGE OF THE *MINOTAUR*, BUT HAUNTED, LIKE A *WOUNDED ANIMAL!*

O BE IT!

THOU ART MY *GREATEST FAILURE,* DIANA OF THEMYSCIRA!

THE PATH THOU HAST *CHOSEN,* NOW THOU SHALL *WALK ALONE!*

FWOOOM

RRRRRR

!

THE MONSTER RISEN LOOMS OVER A DEFENSELESS *DIANA,* ITS FETID BREATH *POUNDING* THE PRINCESS!

WHAT IS THAT I SEE IN ITS *EYES* NOW? IS THAT...

RESPECT?

WE'LL *NEVER* KNOW, FOR TH[E] BEAST TURNS AND SHUFFLES OFF BACK TO IT[S] INFERNAL ABYS[S!]

WHAT A LESSON I'VE LEARNED! I CANNOT WAIT TO TELL MY *SISTERS*-- IF I *EVER* GET BACK TO--

--THEMYSCIRA?! THEN I'M NOT ON *CRETE,* WAR FOOLED ME!

...OR *DID* HE?

IT FEELS RIGHT, SPARING THE *MINOTAUR...*

OR AM I JUST *FOOLING* MYSELF?

CAN MY *MERCY* BE A *TRIBUTE* FOR MY *MOTHER?*

The End?

DOCTOR...

YOU WERE RIGHT.

NO. I WAS WRONG. THIS IS *SOONER* THAN MY CALCULATIONS...

WE'RE NOT *READY,* DAMMIT!

WELL WE HAVE TO BE-- THAT'S HIM, ISN'T IT?

DUERSON-- *NO!* HE DOESN'T UNDERSTAND OUR LANGUAGE!

WE COME IN PEACE--*LOOK,* I HAVE NO *WEAPONS!*

⟨ᛏᚱᚨ ᚦᛟᚺᚺᚢᚢᛗ ᚤᛏᚱ⟩

WE'VE BEEN *WAITING* FOR YOU!

WE'RE HERE TO--

CHEW
CHEW
CHEW
CHEW

...HELP?

I AM THE ONE WITH NO NAME.

THE CRIPPLER OF SOULS...

THE FIRST BORN.

"I DON'T *NEED* YOUR HELP."

OLYMPUS.

MAN, APOLLO'S GOT A LOT OF NERVE...

NO MORE THAN THE *REST* OF US, DIONYSUS.

REALLY? *YOU* WOULD HAVE RAISED A NEW OLYMPUS IF YOU TOOK ZEUS' THRONE?

ME? NO...

I WOULD HAVE *RAZED* IT.

WHOA!

WHAT ARE YOU DRINKING, WAR?

SPOILS, DIO.

SPOILED, MORE LIKE IT.

AH, THAT'S THE LAST OF US. GOOD.

REALLY? I SEE EMPTY CHAIRS...

AND *YOU*, SMITH, SURPRISINGLY.

I CAME BECAUSE WE ARE FAMILY, WAR.

ONE OF THE TWO THINGS WE SHARE.

I DIDN'T ASK ALL OF THE TWELVE TO BE HERE, WAR. JUST US, WHO SHARE THE SAME FATHER.

WHERE'S ATHENA?

SHE...

SHE WON'T RECOGNIZE MY TWIN'S ASCENT TO HEAVEN'S THRONE. SHE *REFUSED* OUR INVITATION.

SO NO *JUSTICE*, THEN, EH, APOLLO?

MY ORACLES GAVE ME A GRAVE PROPHECY, IN TWO PARTS.

THE *FIRST* BEING THAT THERE IS WAR LOOMING THAT THREATENS ALL OF US...

AND SECOND, THAT A CHILD OF ZEUS WOULD SLAY ONE OF US, AND TAKE A THRONE FOR THEMSELVES.

WE ARE NOT THE ONLY CHILDREN OF ZEUS.

WE *ARE* THE MOST POWERFUL.

WE ALREADY HAVE *OUR* THRONES, APOLLO. I THINK YOU'RE SAFE.

I WOULD HAVE AGREED, HAD I NOT WITNESSED ANOTHER OF FATHER'S CHILDREN DISPLAY POWER IN A WAY THAT WOULD PUT THE LION TO SHAME.

BROTHER...

MOON'S BRUISES SPEAK LOUDER THAN MY WORDS, NO?

WHO *DID* THAT?

THE LAST *AMAZON.*

DIANA OF THEMYSCIRA...

LONDON.

HOW YOU DOING, LENNOX?

DAFT POWER, ORGANIC STONE.

I'M CRACKED, BUT I'LL HEAL.

WHAT ABOUT ZOLA?

HEALIN' SAME AS ME, I RECKON.

IT'S NOT GOING TO BE EASY TO FIND HER BABY.

I MEAN, WHEN HERMES WAS WITH US, WE HAD THE POWER OF A GOD TO NAVIGATE ACROSS THE WORLD. WE DON'T HAVE THAT ANYMORE.

NO...BUT PERHAPS WE CAN CALL ON A DEMIGOD?

UGH, I HATE REFERRING TO US THAT WAY...

SEE, DIANA, ZEUS HAD SEVEN KIDS IN THE TWENTIETH CENTURY-- YOU BEING THE LAST TO BE REVEALED.

THERE'S ONE--MAYBE TWO--THAT CAN HELP.

WHY NOT ALL?

ALL AIN'T SO NICE.

BY MY WORD!

I KNOW IT'S HARD FOR YOU TO UNDERSTAND WHY I BROUGHT HERA HERE, BUT NOW A *MORTAL*, SHE'S DEFENSELESS...

YOU SHOULD HAVE LEFT HER TO *DIE!*

PERHAPS, FOR *YOUR* SAKE. BUT FOR MY SISTERS...

AND FOR MY *MOTHER...* I NEED HER TO STAY ALIVE.

IDIOT.

WHY YOU--

ALL RIGHT, *ENOUGH,* THEN.

LOOK, DIANA, THE ONE I WAS SPEAKIN' OF--HER NAME IS *SIRACCA*-- THE WIND.

SHE HEARS ALL THAT IS SAID, AN' SHE TALKS TO ME, CONSTANTLY.

ONLY NOW, SHE WON'T.

DON'T *TRUST* YOU, MY TAKE.

ME? WHY?

THIS VENGEFUL LADY HERE. LIKE I SAYS, WERE *SEVEN* KIDS...

ONLY *FIVE* REMAIN ALIVE.

SIRACCA WON'T *COME* TO YOU.

SO I HAVE TO GO TO HER. WHERE?

LIBYA.

WE'RE SAFE HERE.

YES. WE NOW HAVE PLENTY OF FOOD, WATER... COUPLED WITH THE AMMUNITION...

LET'S CALL IT SAFE.

FOR A CHANGE.

COLONEL--

A WOMAN APPROACHES...

A WOMAN?

WHY, I...

"...WONDER?"

OPEN FIRE!

SHUWOOOSH

CLANK

CLANG CLANK

OH MY...

THIS PLACE.

IT'S WHERE WE HIDE WHEN WE'RE AFRAID.

WELL THEN, WE SHOULD GO TELL YOUR PEOPLE THAT THE SOLDIERS ARE GONE...

AND THERE'S NOTHING TO BE AFRAID OF, SHOULDN'T WE?

SHWWOOOSH

SLAM

WIIIEEE!

SHH, LITTLE ONE...

I WILL PROTECT YOU.

WOW...

YOU HAVE QUITE A PLACE TO HIDE.

ONCE IT WASN'T HERE, AND THEN IT WAS...

WHEN I FOUND IT.

YOU?

YES. IT WAS ONCE THE PALACE OF A KING AND HIS MANY QUEENS. BUT THEY'RE DEAD AND GONE, NOT EVEN GHOSTS.

SIRACCA LIVES HERE NOW.

SIRACCA?

ANTARCTICA.

"WHAT'S HE DOING?"

NOTHING. HE HASN'T MOVED IN OVER SIX HOURS.

CASSANDRA... IS IT TRUE THAT HE ATE DOCTOR DUERSON'S BRAIN?

TO LEARN OUR LANGUAGE, MR. BUTLER.

IS THAT POSSIBLE?

IT HAPPENED.

HE SAID HE DIDN'T NEED OUR HELP.

"HE NEEDS TO BE CONVINCED *OTHERWISE.*"

CAN I ASK--

DO *NOT* DISTURB ME...

OF COURSE. THAT WASN'T MY INTENTION.

IT'S JUST THAT...IT SEEMS YOU'RE *WAITING* FOR SOMETHING.

AND *WAITING*-- AFTER BEING BURIED FOR NEARLY *SEVEN* MILLENNIA...

HOW LONG?

EXACTLY? I CAN *ROUGHLY* ESTIMATE HOW LONG YOU WERE ENTOMBED.

NO. *DIGGING*...

FROM THIS *ROCK'S* MOLTEN PIT, TO ITS *FROZEN* SURFACE. *CLAWING* MY WAY OUT...

SEVEN *THOUSAND* YEARS?

YOU'RE FROM A VANISHED AGE THAT WE KNOW LITTLE ABOUT.

IT'S A PUZZLE THAT HISTORIANS TRY TO PUT TOGETHER WITHOUT MOST OF THE PIECES.

YOUR PIECE, INTENTIONALLY WIPED AWAY.

MY FATHER'S DOING...

YES, HE AND HIS BROTHERS. *FIRST BORN*...

"...OF ZEUS."

SIRACCA--NO! I DON'T WISH TO FIGHT!

AND WHY, WONDER WOMAN, ARE *YOUR* WISHES ANY CONCERN OF MINE?

WHUMP

A CHILD'S LIFE MAY BE AT STAKE!

ARE YOU *MOCKING* ME? A *CHILD'S* LIFE?

LET ME *TELL* YOU ABOUT A CHILD'S LIFE...

PALESTINE. 1917.

"...MY LIFE."

MY, AREN'T YOU PRETTY, LITTLE GIRL...

WHY THANK YOU... ?

NO, YOU DON'T KNOW ME. MY NAME IS HERA, AND I KNOW YOUR FATHER.

REALLY? I'VE NEVER MET HIM--

WOOOOSH

DEAR CHILD...

THERE SEEMS TO BE A STORM APPROACHING...

"THE STORM IS HERE."

SHE DID. IS THAT *DELIGHT* I NEED TO SMACK OFF YOUR STUNNING FACE, APHRODITE?

MOON... I *AM* DELIGHTED. BUT IT'S NOT DIRECTED AT YOU. IT'S A REFLECTION OF WHAT I GLIMPSED-- A *SMILE* ON WAR'S DOUR COUNTENANCE.

I'M AMUSED. SO WHAT?

WELL, LET'S START WITH THIS *NOT* BEING AMUSING. WONDER WOMAN MAY POSE A THREAT.

SHE'S NOT THE ONE WHO'S POSING, APOLLO.

AND AS FOR A *THREAT*-- YOU MEAN TO YOU-- NOT *US*.

THOUGH THAT'S WHAT *YOU* WANT US TO BELIEVE.

YOUR ORACLES SAID A CHILD OF ZEUS WOULD MURDER ANOTHER AND TAKE THEIR THRONE.

AND *AS ONE*, I WOULD HAPPILY MURDER YOU ALL.

"IT'S TIME."

HERA IS NOT TO BE TRUSTED, WONDER WOMAN...

BUT YOU ARE.

SO YOU'LL HELP ME, SIRACCA?

IF HERMES SPEAKS OF THE CHILD YOU SEEK, I WILL HEAR HIM.

HOW IS THAT POSSIBLE?

WORDS ARE CARRIED ON THE WIND, SISTER.

I'M SORRY, BUT THERE'S NOTHING. HE'S EITHER NOT SPEAKING, OR HE HIDES IN A PLACE BEYOND ME.

PERHAPS OUR BROTHER *MILAN* CAN HELP.

THOUGH HE CAN BARELY HELP HIMSELF.

WHERE IS HE?

NEW YORK.

WONDER WOMAN, PLEASE TELL LENNOX THAT I'M SORRY. THAT I WAS *WRONG.*

SISTER... I THINK OUR BROTHER... HE'D LIKE TO HEAR THAT FROM YOU.

"HIGHFATHER..."

WHO'S HUNGRY? I'M HUNGRY.

WHAT HAVE WE HERE, WHAT HAVE WE HERE...?

ONE MAN'S TRASH...

WITH AVOCADO SUPER FOOD.

ROCK ON.

SAY RAH...

EAT FRESH.

IT'S BEEN A WHILE, MY FRIEND...

DON'T MAKE ME DON'T MAKE ME...

I DON'T WANT TO *MAKE* YOU DO ANYTHING, MY FRIEND...

IT'S JUST... YOUR *ABILITY*...

IS A *CURSE!*

YOU DON'T ASK ME FOR HELP, YOU TELL ME WONDERFUL STORIES OF A PLACE I WANT TO *BE* BECAUSE IT IS HEAVEN AND THAT'S WHERE YOU'RE FROM.

I CAN'T I CAN'T I CAN'T...

PERHAPS LATER, THEN.

AFTER A JOYRIDE?

SURE. AFTER A JOYRIDE.

ROCK ON!

SO WHERE DO I FIND OUR BROTHER?

I, DIANA? NOT A GOOD IDEA. MILAN... A NASTY PIECE A WORK, 'E IS.

BARELY CAN STAND *ME*, AN' I'M AS CHARMING AS THEY COME.

HA.

LOOK, 'AVIN' ZEUS AS YOUR DAD--THAT POWER IN THE BLOOD--IT DON' ALWAYS FLOW *CORRECTLY.*

AS YOU KNOW.

AN' I KNOW MILAN, AN' 'E WON'T LIKE YOU WITHOUT A PROPER INTRODUCTION.

EVEN THEN, CHANCES ARE WE'LL GET NOTHING OUT OF 'IM.

SO I GO ALONE.

YOU BABYSIT HER ROYAL HIGH-ASS AN' ZOLA THIS TIME.

WHERE YOU...?

ALL THE DRAMA ABOUT KLOE'S FATHER, I MEAN SERIOUSLY...

KLIK

MY MOTHER-- SHE'S ABSOLUTELY THE B--

--ICH DRIVER WILL BE COMING OUT AHEAD ON THE FOURTH TURN...

KLIK

BARRING ANY MIS--

--UNDERSTANDING, AND THAT'S WHAT YOU WANT OUT OF A MANAGER.

KLIK

OR A MOTHER--

KA--

--LIK

BONK

STOP IT!

SHE STARTED IT.

=SIGH=
I'M SORRY I LOST MY TEMPER.

ZOLA, I NEED YOU TO DO ME A FAVOR...

MAKE SURE HERA DOESN'T LEAVE. YOU'RE IN CHARGE.

WHAT?

THIS CITY WILL EAT YOU ALIVE.

AND HERA, I NEED *YOU* TO DO A FAVOR FOR ME AS WELL.

YOU ARE OUT OF YOUR *MIND*. I'M THE *QUEEN*--

--AND YOU SHALL BE TREATED AS SUCH...

IF YOU ORDER *ROOM SERVICE*. EVERYTHING YOU WANT WILL BE BROUGHT TO YOU, ON A SILVER PLATTER. PLEASE...

INDULGE YOURSELF.

LENNOX...

"...LET'S GO."

OUR BROTHER... HE'S IN *THERE*?

I TOL' YOU HE WASN'T *RIGHT*.

YOU LET HIM LIVE IN--

I DON' *LET* HIM DO ANYTHING-- WHY YOU THINK I 'AVE CONTROL OVER THIS?

MAYBE BECAUSE I LET YOU HAVE SOME CONTROL OVER ME.

WELL, I'M YOUR BIG BROTHER, RIGHT?

PECKING ORDER THING, I RECKON.

AN' DIANA...?

YOU DON' 'AVE TO SAY I HAVE CONTROL OVER YOU. WE BOTH KNOW IT AIN'T TRUE...

THERE BE *OLDER* POWERS IN PLAY.

HUH. IT'S ALMOST LIKE HE *KNEW* I WAS HERE.

HEPHAESTUS?

TOO BAD LENNOX IS NOT THAT CLEVER.

HE *THINKS* HE IS, THOUGH.

WHAT ARE YOU TALKING ABOUT?

AN AMUSING WEAKNESS, THAT ALL OLDER BROTHERS SHARE.

WILL YOU HOLD OUT YOUR ARMS?

WHAT FOR?

MY AMUSEMENT.

THANK YOU.

I MADE THESE, YOU KNOW.

MY MOTHER TOLD ME...

AND SOME THINGS SHE *DIDN'T*...

SHE...

ALWAYS SPOKE--OR *DIDN'T* SPEAK--FROM HER HEART.

YOU SHOULD NEVER FORGET THAT.

WHAT ARE YOU DOING?

JUST TINKERING. THINGS I MAKE, I'M NEVER DONE WITH.

I TRY TO MAKE THEM *BETTER*...

IN CASE THINGS GET WORSE.

WHAT DID YOU DO?

TINKERED. AT THE END OF THE DAY...

"THAT'S ALL GODS DO."

BLOODY HELL...

WHY I ALWAYS STICK MYSELF WITH THE 'ORRID JOBS?

LENNOX?

S'RIGHT, MILAN. IS ME.

I THINK YOU SHOULD GO AWAY.

I'D DO THAT IF I WERE YOU.

WELL, YER NOT. I DON' RUN AWAY FROM PROBLEMS.

IS THIS ONE...IS IT AS BAD AS LAST TIME?

C'MON, I WAS JUS' LOOKIN' FOR OUR SISTER...

I SAW WHAT YOU DID TO HER.

AH...THAT. COULDN'T BE HELPED. TOO MANY LIVES AT STAKE.

ANYWAY, IT ENDED WELL.

NOT FOR EVERYONE.

LITTLE BROTHER, CUT US SOME SLACK. WAS SEVENTEEN YEARS AGO.

YOU *HURT* HER.

I DID-- AN' I KNOW SHE WAS A FAVORITE OF YOURS, BUT...

IT WASN'T *PERSONAL.*

GO AWAY GO AWAY *GO AWAY.*

MILAN... YA DAFT GIT. YA CAN'T *MAKE* ME.

I CAN.

"DREADFUL."

WHAT?

I SAID **DREADFUL**, YOU AWFUL THING.

THIS FOOD...

IT'S NOT GOOD?

NO, IT'S DREADFUL.

GOOD.

WHY DO YOU TAKE SO MUCH JOY FROM MY MISERY?

MAYBE BECAUSE YOU TRIED TO KILL ME. A BUNCH OF TIMES.

YOU LAY DOWN WITH MY HUSBAND. WHAT ELSE AM I SUPPOSED TO DO?

HOW 'BOUT KILL **HIM**?

WHAT? MY **HUSBAND**, THE KING OF THE GODS? I'M HIS **QUEEN**... WHY?

BECAUSE **I** DIDN'T CHEAT ON YOU-- **HE** DID.

--AYE!

YA WANT ME BLIND AS YOU?

HE WANTS YOU TO *LEAVE*...

I DON'T WANT YOU TO *TRIP* ON YOUR WAY OUT.

WELL AIN'T YOU KIND...

LOVELY PLACE YA GOT HERE, DEAR BROTHER.

A REGULA' SANCTUM STANKTORU'

WE DON'T GET ALONG.

GO FIGURE.

YEA...AN' THOUGH YOU CUT QUITE A *DASHING* ONE, THIS BIT BETWEEN ME AN' MILAN IS *FAMILY*, SPACEMAN...

"SO BE POLITE TO OUR *SISTER* ON YOUR WAY OUT."

"OUR *SISTER*, LENNOX? SIRACCA--? OR--"

ONE OF THE TWENTIETH-CENTURY BROOD YOU *HAVEN'T* MET YET.

SIX OF US ACCOUNTED FOR--

YOU FOUND THE LAST ONE?

WHAT?

WHERE?

WHO?

THE *LAST OF THE LINE?!*

YOU AND YOUR *STUPID DAMN* RIDDLES!

MILAN...

CALL OFF YOUR DOG.

YOU HAVE NO IDEA WHAT KIND OF *DANGER* YOU'RE IN!

YOU KNOW WHAT I DO TO MEN LIKE YOU?

IT BETTER BE NOTHING...

"I'M SORRY..."

OVERCOMPENSATING.

?!?

HAVE YOU NO--

SHLUCK

RESPECT?

YOUR COMPREHENSION OF ME IS AS STUNTED AS YOUR GROWTH.

WELL, THEN...

I LOOK FORWARD TO HEARING YOU WAIL ABOUT YOURSELF...

FOR ETERNITY!

WHUMP

Y'KNOW SOMETHING, MY LEFT *HOOK* AND YOUR STONE HEAD ARE ABOUT TO BE...

NO FIGHTING. OKAY.

MY NAME IS *ORION*. I'M NOT FROM EARTH-- *OBVIOUSLY*-- I JUST COME HERE TO *RELAX*.

BUT RECENTLY I'VE LEARNED OF A THREAT TO THE UNIVERSE. THAT THE END OF TIME BEGINS WITH *THE LAST OF THE LINE*...

AT THE HANDS OF A NEW *GOD*.

A NEW GOD. YOU THINK...?

ZOLA'S BABY.

IT SEEMS WE'RE HERE FOR THE SAME REASON. WE KNOW OF THIS "NEW GOD" YOU'RE AFTER. OUR FRIEND, SHE'S THE MOTHER.

BUT IT WAS STOLEN FROM HER, NEWLY BORN...

BY AN *OLD* GOD.

WAIT A MINUTE-- THE THREAT TO THE UNIVERSE IS A *CHILD*?

WELL, IT HAS HAPPENED BEFORE...

BUT I'VE BEEN SENT TO BATTLE AN *INFANT!?!*

HMMM.

I STAND CORRECTED.

FROM THE LOOKS OF YOU, IT APPEARS YOU CHEATED ME ONCE...

FROM THE LOOKS OF ME...

UNDERSTAND SHE'LL CHEAT YOU TWICE.

YOUR FATHER'S BARGAIN... IT WAS A FOOL'S!

THAT FOOL...

ME HERE...

...MEANS HE'S NOT.

OLYMPUS...

I'M COMING FOR YOU!!!

THAT'S SOMETHING *LEARNED.*

WE NEED TO MAKE SURE THIS BABY ISN'T TAUGHT THAT WAY.

BUT I DO KNOW A CHILD IS NEVER BORN BAD.

WE ARE BORN MANY DIFFERENT WAYS, THAT MIGHT BE DIFFICULT... THAT WE *STRUGGLE* WITH. BUT BAD...

LENNOX TOLD ME YOU HAVE THE POWER TO HELP US.

DON'T MAKE ME DON'T MAKE ME

DIANA, YOU'RE WASTING YOUR TIME. HE'S CRAZY--

IN *PAIN,* LENNOX. HE'S IN PAIN. AND HE'S MY BROTHER.

NEW SISTER... YOU ARE A NICE NEW SISTER.

A BAD BABY IS A BAD IDEA

LET ME *SEE* IF I CAN HELP YOU.

THE QUEEN OF ROOTS.

WHO?

AAAH!

STARRY EYES! BIRD MAN! TREE LADY?...

DEMETER. HERMES IS HIDING THE BABY WITH DEMETER.

BUT I HAVE NO IDEA WHERE THAT COULD BE.

S'A GOOD THING YOU KEEP YOUR ENEMIES CLOSE...

AH. I *TOLD* YOU HERA WOULD COME IN HANDY.

STARRY STARRY EYES...

WHAT IS THAT, MILAN?

THE BABY...

SAW ME...

SO, ZOLA...

YOUR CHILD... IT MAY BRING THE END OF TIME.

WHAT'S *THAT* SUPPOSED TO MEAN?

WELL, THE END. OF *EVERYTHING.* LIFE--THE AFTERLIFE-- DONE AND GONE.

THEN IT HAS TO *DIE!*

I KNEW YOU'D SAY THAT, HERA. BECAUSE KILLING AN INFANT IS SO...

COMMON FOR YOU? --BUT FOR *ME*, IT'S-- OH, COMMON, TOO-- I MEAN I'M AN *AMAZON*--

WHAT *ARE* YOU DOING?

FIGURING OUT HOW TO SAY WHAT I NEED TO SAY *BEFORE* I SAY IT.

HUH. YOU DON'T STRIKE ME AS A WOMAN WHO THINKS BEFORE SHE SPEAKS.

AN' THA'S A STRIKE AGAINST YOU, SPACEMAN.

MY *NAME* IS ORION...

OH...

...KAY.

STOP.

LOOK... I DON'T NEED YOU TWO BICKERING. I'VE ALREADY GOT THESE--

?

ZOLA? HERA?

ANYONE?!

IT APPEARS THE BIRDS HAVE FLOWN THE COOP.

BUT I TOLD THEM TO STAY HERE!

MUST NOT OF HEARD YEA...

LENNOX, DO YOU HAVE ANY IDEA HOW *BIG* THIS CITY IS-- AND THEY COULD BE *ANYWHERE* IN IT?

YES.

AND MAYBE-- MAYBE THEY *DIDN'T* LEAVE, BUT WERE *TAKEN*?

YES.

AND THAT IT'S *YOUR* FAULT?

COME AGAIN?

IF YOU HAD STAYED HERE AND LET ME GO BY *MYSELF*--

HOL' *ON* A MINUTE-- Y'KNOW, YOU CONTINUE WITH THIS "I'LL HANDLE THINGS ALONE" RUBBISH, ALL THE WHILE COLLECTING A MOTLEY CREW THAT YOU KEEP ADDING TO!

WELL LOOK, SISTER--AN' NO, I *DON'* MEAN THAT IN THE FAMILY SENSE-- YOU *DON'* GET IT BOTH WAYS!

THIS MOTLEY CREW...

IS ONE OF THEM *BLONDE?*

"ZOLA..."

...LET *ME* HANDLE THIS.

STRIFE! WHAT A SURPRISE!

OH COME NOW, DIO.

SELF-INDULGE AND I GO H. IN HAND.

MOTHE

STRIFE?

ᔓKISSᔔ ᔓKISSᔔ

OOH.

WHAT?

I WAS GOING TO ASK YOU WH IT WAS LIKE TO *MORTAL...*

BUT THOSE LITTLE WRINKLES AROUND YOUR EYES ARE *ALL* THE ANSWER I NEED.

HELLO, WAR.

...YOU FED A HAIR INTO YOUR MACHINE AND IT WAS ABLE TO LOCATE THE HEAD IT CAME OFF?

I FED A MACHINE HAIR... SOMETHING LIKE THAT, SURE.

WHY, LOOK WHO IT IS! THE DAY IS--

OOH...

AND YOU ARE...?

I AM CALLED OR--

--STOP!

DON'T STOP.

STRIFE... I SHOULD HAVE KNOWN YOU WERE BEHIND THIS.

NO, BABY SISTER... BEHIND ME BE YOUR "THIS."

ZOLA, I CAN'T BELIEVE...

...IT'S YOU. KNOW I LOOK A SHADE DIFFERENT FROM LAST WE MET, BUT THEN, SO DO YOU...

LITTLE ONE.

WONDER WOMAN, RUN! HE'S HERE TO KILL--

ANAK KRAKATAU.

"TELL ME, CASSANDRA..."

ABOUT YOUR NECK. THE ARMOR...

IT'S NOT ARMOR, FIRST BORN...

IT *IS* MY NECK, AND IT'S NOT BY MY CHOICE.

A MACHINE, THEN. LIKE THE ONE WE'RE IN.

THE WORLD IS NOTHING LIKE IT WAS WHEN...YOU HAVE A *LOT* TO LEARN.

AND *YOU* HAVE DECIDED TO TEACH ME.

WHY?

I HAVE MY REASONS.

I WANT TO...LEARN THEM.

ARE YOU A GOD?

YES.

THEN WHY *SHOULDN'T* I SERVE YOU?

HMM.

YOU CAN KEEP YOUR SECRETS. THEY REALLY DON'T MATTER, THOUGH.

BECAUSE IT'S TRUE.

BECAUSE I *AM* A GOD.

MY WEAPONS...

?

WHY DO YOU SAY THAT?

"YOUR WEAP... ARE BURIE... IN A MOUNTA... ACTUALLY... A VOLCANO..."

THAT DOESN'T MAKE SENSE. IF MY *SKIN* WAS GIVEN TO HELL, THEN MY *STRENGTH* HAD TO BE GIVEN TO THE *SEA*.

LIKE I SAID, THE WORLD HAS CHANGED. WHAT WAS ONCE UNDERWATER IS NOW--

HOLY--

"HERMES TOOK THE BABY TO DEMETER."

THE THIEF IS *CLEVER.* TAKING THE CHILD TO HARVEST IS HIDING IT THE FIRST PLACE ANYONE SHOULD LOOK.

WELL, ANYONE WITH *WITS.*

I *WON'T* TAKE YOU THERE.

WHAT--HERA? AFTER I'VE TAKEN YOU UNDER MY--

IT *SOUNDS* LIKE SHE'S REFUSING, BUT...

MOTHER'S MORTAL NOW. ONLY *OLYMPIANS* CAN MOVE BETWEEN REALMS UNINVITED.

SO *YOU* CAN'T, EITHER?

I HATE THE SILLY RULES, TOO--BUT I *WILL* TAG ALONG.

NOT ON *MY* WATCH.

...YOU *WILL* TAKE US?

OF COURSE NOT.

I'LL TAKE YOU.

DIANA, YOU CAN'T *TRUST* THIS MAN. WHAT IF HE'S THE ONE THAT WILL MAKE THE CHILD EVIL?

LUMMOX, HE'S THE ONLY ONE THAT CAN *GET* HER THERE.

SO GO AT IT.

SLAP

WHAT THE--

--HELL DO YOU THINK YOU'RE ALL *DOING?!*

IT'S *MY* BABY--AND YOU ACT LIKE I'M NOT EVEN HERE!

...A...I'M SORRY. SOMETIMES I AKE CONTROL OF HINGS--AND IT'S ONTROLLING, I KNOW...

...BUT NLY WANT BRING YOUR ABY BACK TO YOU.

THIS IS THE BEST CHANCE I--*WE'VE* GOT.

CAN I DO THIS FOR YOU?

PERHAPS I SHOULD GO ALONE AND GET IT MYSELF.

DON'T LET THAT HAPPEN.

IT PAINS ME, LITTLE ONE, TO FIND YOU NO BETTER OFF THAN WHEN I LEFT YOU ALL THOSE YEARS AGO...

OR FOR THAT MATTER, NO *WORSE.*

I DON' WANT Y HELP, W

BUT YO NEED I

AND "ALL THOSE YEARS"...IT WAS ONLY *TEN.* ISN'T THAT JUST A DROP IN THE BUCKET FOR YOU?

...JUST TEN YEARS. *HMM.* SEEMS LONGER. MY LIFE...

IT'S LIKE I EXPERIENCE IT IN REVERSE.

WHEN I WAS YOUNG, THE DAYS WERE MEASURED IN THE NIGHTS. NOW THAT I'M OLD...

THEY WON'T END.

WHERE ARE YOU GOING?

THE BARTENDER MENTIONED THAT THEY HAVE A ROOFTOP GARDEN.

I BET *THAT'S* SOMETHING TO SEE...

SO LET'S.

I'M NOT THE SAME AS YOU LEFT ME, WAR.

REALLY?

THE QUEEN OF ROOTS

GORAN SUDŽUKA artist (pages 4-5, 8-10, 13-17)   **CLIFF CHIANG** artist (pages 18-20)
TONY AKINS with **DAN GREEN** layouts and finishes (pages 1-3, 6-7, 11-12)

DON'T
T TO FIGHT,
HERMES.

WHAT *IS* IT YOU
WANT?

THE
BABY.

I'M GOING TO *HAVE TO* FIGHT,
AREN'T I?

"YOUR THREATS ARE *MEANINGLESS*,
POSEIDON!"

KLANG

YOUR SKILLS ARE IMPRESSIVE, DIANA...

I HAD THE GREATEST TEACHERS IN THE WORLD.

KLANG

KLANG

I AM AN AMAZON...

AND T
DAUGH
OF A G

SEEMS, THOUGH...

THWACK

YOU HAVEN'T LEARNED THE DANCE.

SPEED CAN'T BE TAUGHT.

AND THERE IS NO ONE FASTER THAN I.

YOU CAME IN MY HOUSE WITH A PURPOSE. BUT THINKING ME WOUNDED...

MY WELL-BEING BECAME MORE IMPORTANT.

NO WONDER WAR HATES YOU.

PERHAPS MORE THAN HE HATES HIMSELF.

THERE WAS A TIME WHEN THE SONGS OF WAR WOULD ECHO THROUGH OLYMPUS...

HIS VOICE... IT WAS GLORIOUS.

NOW, IT'S LITTLE MORE THAN A RASP. LIKE LOCUST WINGS, RUBBING AGAINST DEAD WOOD.

HE RIPPED ME OPEN AND TOOK THE BABY.

AND I LET HIM DO IT.

YOU *LET* HIM?

I COULDN'T STOP HIM...

"NOW GO."

HOW COULD I HAVE BEEN SO STUPID?!

YOU'RE ASKING ME? I JUST MET YOU. FOR ALL I KNOW, THIS IS THE WAY YOU ALWAYS--

I WAS AN IDIOT TO TRUST WAR!

BUT YOU DIDN'T TRUST HIM, DID YOU?

HFFFF... I TOOK A CHANCE. I NEEDED TO RESCUE THAT BABY.

STILL DO. SO STOP BEATING YOURSELF UP.

STOP?! DO YOU HAVE ANY IDEA HOW BAD THIS IS? A CHILD YOU YOURSELF SAID WOULD END TIME-- IN THE HANDS OF WAR?

UM...AS BAD AS IT SOUNDS?

LOOK, IT WASN'T A CHANCE, IT WAS A RISK. AND GIVEN THE STAKES, YOU DID RIGHT TAKING IT.

NOT THIS TIME...

THAT'S WHAT NEXT TIMES ARE FOR.

WE'LL FIND THEM.

THANK YOU.

Y'KNOW, YOU'RE KINDA CUTE WHEN YOU GET MAD.

UGH...

EVERYONE...

WHAT'S WRONG?

WHAT ISN'T?

DIANA?

ZOLA-- ARE YOU...

HE BROUGHT MY BABY BACK.

WAR?

YOU OWE ME, LITTLE ONE.

IF YOU MEAN AN APOLOGY, THEN...

I WAS WRONG ABOUT 'IM, DIANA.

OH, LENNOX, BUT YOU WEREN'T...

DIANA, DO YOU WANT TO HOLD...

ORION

ASTRO HARNESS

CLIFF
CHIANG
2012
ORION II A

Orion by Jim Lee

SIROCCA

CLIFF
CHIANG
2012

CLIFF CHANG 2012

DIONYSUS

FIRST BORN

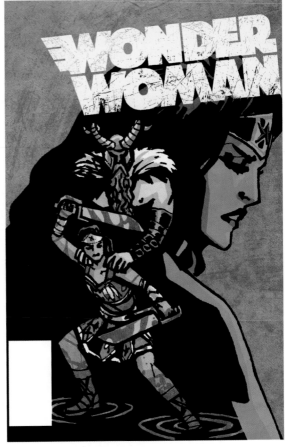

BORN ON A HIDDEN ISLAND PARADISE AND RAISED BY A FIERCE TRIBE OF AMAZON WARRIORS, PRINCESS DIANA IS THE DAUGHTER OF QUEEN HIPPOLYTA AND THE KING OF THE GODS, ZEUS! TO THE REST OF THE WORLD, SHE IS THE HERO KNOWN AS... **WONDER WOMAN!**

THE LAIR OF THE MINOTAUR!

CREDITS

WONDER WOMAN #0 - "LAIR OF THE MINOTAUR!"

PAGE 1- Splash, natch.
We open with young Diana scaling a sheer cliff. The wind buffets her. She's climbing towards a nest — one with eggs in it. Below her, the crashing surf. It's daytime.

PAGES 2-3
Reaching the nest, she grabs one of the eggs. Suddenly, a Harpy comes swooping down at her. Holy crap — those are harpy eggs! Diana avoids the sharp talons, then dives off the nest, cradling the egg. She plummets down off the cliff. Just before the harpy can reach her, Diana rolls and hits the water. Under the water, Diana swims towards a cave. Surfacing in the cave, She is met by her mother and a party of Amazon warriors. The cave is lit only by their torches. There is great rejoicing when she presents her mother with the harpy egg — a gift to commemorate her fourteenth birthday. A bottle of mead is raised in Diana's honor; she will make a fine Amazon. In the dark of the cave, Ares watches. This one... she is special.

PAGES 4-5
Later that night, Themyscira celebrates Diana's birthday with jousting games — much like from Issue #2. Of course Diana is taking part. A young Aleka taunts her, calling her Clay. As they joust, Diana is consumed by thoughts; she is not like her sisters, and she wishes she was. She bests Aleka — and almost goes too far, nearly killing her before Hippolyta puts a stop to it. Realizing what she did, Diana runs off into the forest.

PAGE 6

In the forest she again wonders why she must be different. Ares appears, and answers her question. It is a gift to be different, and he offers to show her how. A brave Diana accepts. Ares tells her to meet him here in the forest each full moon, and he will train her to be a warrior. A white owl watches from the trees...

PAGES 7-8

Montage pages, Ares training Diana in combat, showing her the world, taking her to his weapon room, which is loaded with weapons from many eras (including a Mother Box — very important). The moon is always full in the night sky. Also interspersed is her training with other Amazons — and getting the better of them. Both Hippolyta and Ares smile (different panels, or Ares ghostly — they never see each other.) A year goes by.

PAGE 9

Another training page. They are jousting. Ares shows Diana that a clever warrior knows how to use an enemy's weapon against them. When she thrusts at him, he grabs her arm, and turns her blade on herself. She though, turns it on him; she's managed to rope his ankle with her lasso, and pulls his leg out from under him. Very good, little one, very good. I believe next moon, you are ready for a test.

PAGE 10

Okay, how about another Splash? Ares stands behind a cocky and brave Diana, one hand on her shoulder, the other outstretched before them. She holds her dagger and her lasso. Ares tells her that all she's learned will be put to a great test...

PAGE 11

Reverse POV. "Behold, the lair of the Minotaur, the most fearsome beast known to man or God! It is in this maze that you will prove yourself as a warrior." "I will make you proud, War." "I don't doubt you, little one." Diana heads into the maze.

PAGES 12-13

Diana in the maze. Her thoughts are about making Ares proud of her. She comes across human bones, armor, and weapons — the maze is littered with them. She unfurls her lasso, so she can find her way out. The Minotaur stalks her, following her lasso, maybe? Diana hears something behind her. She turns...

PAGES 14-16

The Minotaur comes charging. The battle is on, and it's hard one for Diana. The Minotaur is all brute force, and it's tough for Diana to mount any offense. Luckily, she remembers her last training session with Ares, "Use your enemy's weapon against them." Diana gets some distance between her and the Minotaur, and backs up against a wall. The beast charges her. Just before it hits, she catapults herself out of the way. The Minotaur runs head down into the wall. It's dazed. Using her hand-to-hand combat training, Diana topples the Minotaur.

PAGE 17

As Diana stands over the struggling beast, Ares appears and hands Diana a sword. "Finish the job. Its head will make a fitting tribute to your mother on this, the day that marks your fifteenth season, my warrior." Diana raises the sword... "Do it!" The Minotaur crawls... "Kill him, little one!" She drops the sword. "I won't kill in cold blood."

PAGE 18

Ares is disgusted with Diana, saying she's not a true warrior — she's failed to see that a dangerous enemy must be killed, because it will come back to haunt — maybe even kill her. He goes on, "I was wrong about you. You are no warrior." She runs to him, begging forgiveness. Ares slaps her away. "You are no student of mine." He disappears.

PAGE 19

The Minotaur rises. Diana struggles to her feet. The beast looks at her, then turns back down a tunnel. It proves Ares wrong.

PAGE 20

Diana exits the maze, as the sun rises. She feels good about herself, yet wonders what the future holds. She knows, though, that their paths will cross again.

END

*"Clear storytelling at its best. It's ar
intriguing concept and easy to grasp."*
—NEW YORK TIMES

*"Azzarello is rebuilding the mythology
of Wonder Woman."*
-MAXIM

START AT THE BEGINNING!

WONDER WOMAN
VOLUME 1: BLOOD

**MR. TERRIFIC
VOLUME 1:
MIND GAMES**

**BLUE BEETLE
VOLUME 1:
METAMORPHOSIS**

**THE FURY OF FIRESTORM:
THE NUCLEAR MEN
VOLUME 1:
GOD PARTICLE**

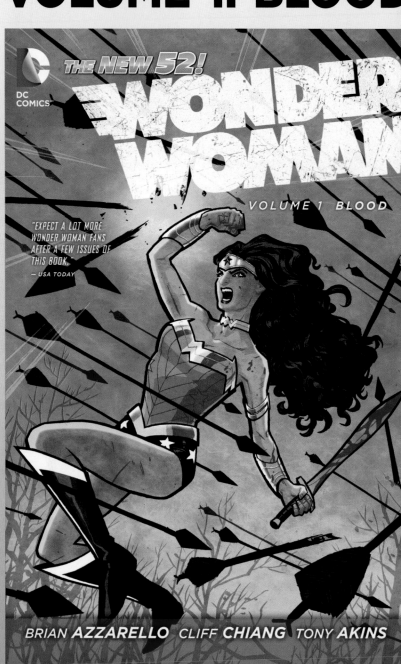

BRIAN **AZZARELLO** CLIFF **CHIANG** TONY **AKINS**